OTHER TITLES BY
KIRK GILCHRIST:

I Plead For Your Children

For Such A Time As This

Out In Front

A Portrait of Heavens Love – *English and Spanish*

For more life resources visit newlifenny.com
or download the newlifenny app
from your mobile device's app store.

IMPACT

WE CAN CHANGE THE WORLD

KIRK GILCHRIST

NEW LIFE BOOKS

IMPACT

Published by Kirk Gilchrist in alliance with New Life Books
255 Gaffney Dr., Watertown, NY 13601 USA

Special thanks Elizabeth Bettger, Harry and Darlene Jensen, Rebekah Berthet

Cover design and interior layout by Jason J Clement | jasonjclement.com

Author photo by Jessica Burt | jovialphotography.format.com

ISBN: 98153569062

Printed in the United States of America

CONTENTS

WE CAN CHANGE THE WORLD

We have been born into an unprecedented time in history. Need is in virtually every nation and the outcry for solution is great. We stand at a time when humanity is pointing its finger at God and asking, "What are you doing? Why are you not stopping the madness that is happening in the world? Why are you letting innocent lives be affected?" These questions are not new and yet the church world has been so consumed with these accusations against God they have missed the alarmingly obvious, and completely attainable answer.

This booklet while prophetic in nature is also pragmatic in its approach. Through its pages we will begin to unwrap the answer that has perplexed generations. Contemplating all these things I am reminded of the words of the prophet Joel.

JOEL 3:9-16 — Proclaim this among the nations: Consecrate for war; stir up the mighty men. Let all the men of war draw near; let them come up. Beat your plowshares into swords, and your pruning hooks into spears; let the weak say, "I am a warrior. Hasten and come, all you surrounding nations, and gather yourselves there, Bring down your warriors, O Lord. Let the nations stir themselves up and come up to the Valley of Jehoshaphat; for there I will sit to judge all the surrounding nations. Put in the sickle, for the harvest is ripe. Go in, tread, for the winepress is full. The vats overflow, for their evil is great. Multitudes, multitudes, in the valley of decision! For the day of the Lord is near in the valley of decision. The sun and the moon are darkened, and the stars withdraw their shining. The Lord roars from Zion, and utters his voice from Jerusalem, and the heavens and the earthquake; But the Lord is a refuge to his people, a stronghold to the people of Israel.

We stand in this moment, but what are we going to do with the time and the resources that we are given? Take a moment to picture our land transformed, our world changed, and even, perhaps a world influenced by Christ followers.

Let us imagine for a moment that we are on a trip to the country of Sudan. You walk up to a village and as you are walking you begin to see smoke, and trees that have been stripped by fire. Your curiosity is peaked and a spark of fear begins to grow in your heart, something is very wrong. Suddenly, you see where the smoke is coming from; They are homes that you can hardly make out as such because their mud walls and thatched grass roofs are now unrecognizable. Standing around the wreckage you see men in shock. The women and the children are crying in both confusion and fear. You begin to ask what happened but for a moment the words will not form in your mind. Finally, your words form but all that you can utter is, "They took them?" "Took who?" Your words are fervent and desperate as you try to make sense of the situation. Then finally, through her tears, one brave woman says, "Our teenage daughters. They took our daughters..." If she said anything after that you did not hear her. The emotion that has risen up inside of you is just too strong to hear anything but the pounding of your own heart against your chest. You know all too well the fate of these innocent ones. Abuse, torment, and ultimately being sold like cattle to the highest bidder in the human sex trafficking trade. By now, you don't know how much more you can take. Slowly, you look up, wipe your tear stained face, and realize how few adults there are left in the village and how many children are running from burned hut to burned hut desperate to find signs of their parents. Once more your heart shatters knowing these little ones will never find what they seek. Unable to take in such destruction, you close your eyes to the horror you are witnessing. You are overwhelmed by the images that have been burned into your mind. Crushed under the weight of the emotion and reality of life here, you fall to your knees too stunned to speak a single word out loud. All that keeps repeating in your head is "How could I have helped? I have to help. What can be done?"

Laying in your bed that night, you can't sleep. Images that you saw that day spill into your thoughts every time you close your eyes. In your restless state, you can't stop thinking, how could I have been so blind to what was happening outside my front door. Suddenly, there is an awakening inside of you. "Why have I never seen this before?" you ask yourself. You know that help has always been a possibility for these precious people. You start to think about the care, commitment, and compassion that is available a world away from the horror you experienced today. The reality sinks in and you think to yourself, "If the church really cared and gave sacrificially, this land can be changed." Finally, you drift off to sleep with the thought in your mind that a world changed by the church would be an amazing thing to see.

Come with me now to Somalia. Here you see a mother, her anemia has reached a tragic level. Her clothing doesn't fully cover her emaciated body and the bones she so desperately wants to hide. You look into her eyes and you are captivated. Your concentration is only broken because of a small sound you hear coming from somewhere next to the woman. You quickly become all too aware that the sound is the labored breathing of a little girl. Lost in this moment, the sound becomes all you can hear. Taking in her tiny form and bloated belly, you realize she will not see the sunrise tomorrow. Her breathing gets harder and harder. You feel helpless. You would give anything to be able to do something for this little girl. You try to yell for someone, anyone to come help her but no one hears. Your ears are filled with the sound of her breath. Your senses are overwhelmed by it. Then suddenly, it is gone. There is silence. The kind of silence that washes over you and screams louder than a thousand sirens. She is gone. Taking a deep breath, you try to compose yourself. You stand up straight, stretch, and look around. In this moment, you realize the reason that all you could hear was labored breathing was not just because of this beloved child you had just watched take her last breath; but, it was because you were surrounded by dozens that were suffering just like her. When you came in the room, you were so focused on her and her mother that you missed the vastness of this epidemic. Astonished, and heart sick you are brought back to your last thought on your last night in the Sudan. What if the church could change the world? What if we, the church, could solve this?

After this trip very emotional trip, you return home but the scenes continue to replay in your mind. So far away, people are suffering in untold misery. As you are sitting in your living room with your thoughts, you can hear the familiar sounds of the children playing outside and cars driving by. As the days drift by, all that pain that you saw starts to fade into a distant memory as you settle back into your routine. Then, suddenly, reality strikes much closer to home. One night around eleven o'clock you hear a frantic knock at the door. You pause your favorite show and go to answer your door. It is your neighbor.

Sweating, gasping for air, and panicked he asks, "Have you seen my daughter? She was playing in the front yard after dinner and we can't find her!"

No, you haven't seen her this evening. Without even thinking, you throw on your shoes and coat and you join in the hunt. The police have been called. The neighborhood has been canvassed, and there is no sign of her. Painstaking weeks pass, you check in with the family and there has been no news. The police are calling off the search. Feeling helpless, you offer a hug. Distraught with feelings of helplessness you return home.

The next morning you get a phone call from your neighbor. He has news on his daughter. The daughter that he loved and cherished. The one that used to giggle and tickle him when she wanted his attention. The one that just last week was playing and laughing in their front year. The conversation with the police officer was a devastating blow to the family.

"Sir," he began, "we have news on your daughter. She was kidnapped from your front yard. We have seen this tactic used before and by the same people. They have sold her from one sex trafficking location to another.

"Then go get her!" my neighbor screamed.

"Sir," continued the officer, "we can't find her. she has been sold multiple times and we have lost the trail of where they have taken her."

Slumping down in your chair the realization hits you... sold...sold...sold, but that is your neighbor's daughter. She ate dinner here. She played with your daughter. You helped her learn how to ride a bike...sold. The same fear and anger that washed over you in the Sudan suddenly hits your chest. You saw and you know the atrocities that were being committed against this seven-year-old girl. Seething with anger against the person who would do such a thing, you realize your neighbor is still on the phonc.

"Hello? Are you still there?"

Coming to, as one woken from a dream, you realize that this could have been your daughter. You have no words to comfort this man, this friend. You find something to say, but afterwards, you can't even remember what it was. As you hang up the phone you realize that a friendly little face is peeking around the corner. Daddy, why are you crying? Without saying a word, you scoop her up in your arms and hold her as close as you can. Without saying a word your heart cries out to God. It could have been my girl. All this time, I've been painting my white picket fence, mowing my lawn, doing life here. I never gave a second thought to the fact that those little girls were being raped, used, sold, and terrorized. They are all someone's daughter. Sitting there in the silence, hugging your little girl, you begin to weep and all that you can see and hear in your imagination is a gavel falling, a man yelling sold, and your little girl standing there on the auction block.

This thought may seem like too much for your heart to bare. However, these stories are realities for millions around the globe. In our very own towns there are lives being taken by drugs, alcohol, and sex-trafficking. Kids living without care, compassion, or love that many other children are given freely. There are schools without the necessary staffing and students falling through the educational cracks.

There are needs everywhere. All this pain, suffering and loss overwhelms our senses and brings the reality too close to home. It makes us want to turn a blind eye and go back to our everyday naive existence. What would happen if, instead of turning a blind eye, we grabbed ahold of the truth that in EVERY situation, there is great hope. There is a light that shines on a hill. A beacon of hope that shines for all that are lost and hurting. That light is the church! It is the sacrificial body of Christ! A body that is living and serving as Jesus with flesh on. It is the church fully buying in, and saying that we are no longer satisfied with the way things are. It's the church with real power and real care actually doing something to change the world.

Let me ask you this: What do you think about when you go to bed at night? What do you think about when you wake up? What do you think about when you're driving to work? What consumes you?

If the church is to be the answer, then what consumes us must switch from the mindset of a consumer to the mindset of giver. Imagine, for a moment, a world that has been radically affected by the giving Christian church of the United States of America!

Here are some alarmingly true facts about the world that we live in today:

Hunger kills more people than AIDS, malaria, and tuberculosis combined. This makes hunger the number one health risk in the world today.

1 in 7 people in the world will go to bed hungry tonight.

Every single day over 300 million children go to bed hungry.

Around 700,000 children die every year from diarrhea caused by unclean water and poor sanitation methods. That is almost 2,000 children a day.

Almost 16,000 children die from hunger-related causes every day. That means this world loses a child every five seconds.

1-2-3-4-5

Someone's child just died.

1-2-3-4-5

Another person's child just died.

1-2-3-4-5

Another person's child just died, and it continues on and on and on. All because of hunger that could have been prevented.

This has to get our attention. It certainly got the attention of Jesus 2,000 years ago. In Matthew 25 Jesus specifically states:

> **MATTHEW 25:40 (ESV)** – "And the King will answer them, 'Truly, I say to you, as you did it to one of the least of these my brothers, you did it to me.'"

I have to wonder how our lives reflect Christ in our treatment of the rest of the world. We must consider that there is a group on this planet that is seen as out-giving, out-committing, and out-working us as Christians. That group is "radical Islam." As Christian's, we need to fully embrace the love of Christ for all mankind and how he has called us to steward this world. Perhaps, the answer to radical Islam is a sold out, radical Christian church that is willing to serve his fellow man according to the word of God. Now, that would be a world changer.

The answer to the world's crisis is where it has **ALWAYS** been...in the local church. That would be you and me, our churches, our giving habits and our real priorities. Jesus said:

> **MATTHEW 6:21** – "Where your treasure is, there your heart will be also."

Jesus himself said that our heart follows our treasure not

the other way around. The Bible also tells us to "seek first," the kingdom of God, and all these things, (houses, cars, lands, etc.) would be added to us. This is truth both amazing and alarming (we will discuss this topic more in depth later in this booklet).

When it comes to finances, there is a stigma that has been put on churches. We have all heard someone say that the church just wants your money or that they are trying to take you for everything you are worth. We have all seen the televangelists on the news that were caught misappropriating funds. They really were trying to get all they could out of people and they were misusing the word of God to do it. This 5% of the church has really painted a bleak picture to the rest of the unbelieving and some of the believing world. This, however, is not the reality for the rest of the 95% of the church leaders today. The majority of leaders in the church today are living sacrificially and handling the finances of the church with the honor, care and respect that is required of them. This is the Lord's money and they treat it as such. These faithful servants of the Lord, which we often just think of as our local staff are vital to the life of the church and the expansion of the cause of Christ. That being said, I believe that we must honor these hard working men and women. This includes honoring them through financial means as well as adding to our staff so that we do not overburden them with the work that needs to be done.

In saying that, it is important to mention that if you are not a part of the church staff now that does not mean that you are not able to do the work of Christ. The church, as a whole, desperately needs volunteers. Now you may be thinking that you are too busy with life right now; but, we have to ask ourselves again...where is our treasure? If you find that, then you will know exactly where your heart is.

The church staff in America is overworked and tired, being a faithful volunteer is the greatest gift you can give to your church. Everyone on this planet has a core drive to do something with their life that will fulfill them and make them a part of something that is bigger than what they could accomplish alone. What better place to make a connection, change a life, and feel valued than in your local church? Have you ever stopped to think about why God placed you in a church in the United States or why this nation is a Christian nation? I believe that this was God's plan all along.

THE FUNDAMENTALS

In this next section we are going to be looking at one of the most fundamental teachings on giving in the Bible. This portion of scripture reveals God's heart in a powerful way. Some may brush this teaching off as minor doctrine, but the implication of Christians buying into the giving heart of God will change this world. It is vitally important that we let the Bible speak to us and teach us. We should never try to force biblical truths into the framework of our doctrine or theology. With the foundation that the Bible can stand alone; and that we are to live by it and not it living by us, we are going to take a look at tithing through the eyes of Malachi 3. This powerful discourse answers the questions that have been purposed to both God and men through the ages.

The answers in this chapter will transform our world; but, only if we first let them transform our hearts.

> MALACHI 3:6 (ESV) – "For I am the Lord and I do not change."

This simple sentence seems so iniquitous, and yet there is tremendous depth within its meaning. God is telling us from the very beginning of this section of scripture that he does not change. God, knowing the beginning from the end, wanted to lay out in the foundations of this truth that what He was about to say was never going to change. He specifically made this statement knowing full well that there were going to be many who contested this portion of scripture, and that they would assert that he had in fact changed. For example, there are people in the church today that believe that because they do not see the concept of tithing explicitly stated in the New Testament that God has changed his mind on tithing. They also believe that it is no longer relevant. This would suggest that God has changed his mind on the concept of tithing. We know, however, that this is false. In Hebrews, we see Jesus talking about tithing in a positive light, thus restating the fact that God, whether Father, Son, or Spirit, does not change.

Not only does God not change his mind, even more importantly, His nature does not change. This is critically important to our belief and understanding. We so often hear Christians saying that they want to look like Christ. When we think that through, what does that look like? The answer to that can be found in this verse:

> JOHN :16 – "For God so loved the world that He gave His only begotten son. That whoever believes in him shall not perish but shall have eternal life through Christ Jesus our Lord."

What does this tell us about our unchanging God? God himself is a giver. So, if we want to be like Him than our destiny is to be givers as well. You may feel yourself shutting down and reverting back to the old way of thinking that the church is just trying to get your money again; but, stop for a moment and just take this in. God is, by nature, a giver. If we presuppose that we are made in the image of God than we can logically come to the conclusion that we too are programed in our very being to be givers as well. This booklet is not just another pastor trying to get your money. This is a word from the heart of God unlocking the purpose that has always been in you. A purpose to give, change the world, and ultimately to be more like Christ.

> MALACHI 3:7-8 – "From the days of your fathers you have turned aside from my statutes and have not kept them. Return to me, and I will return to you, says the LORD of hosts. But you say, 'How shall we return?' Will man rob God? Yet you are robbing me. But you say, 'How have we robbed you?'"

These powerful statements that tell us that we have gone away from God and we have not kept His concepts are very sobering; but, the writer goes even further to say that we have **robbed** God. This daunting scripture deserves our full respect and attention. This is the God who knows everything, sees everything, and whom we will stand before and give account of our lives! What a terrifying thought. I'm overwhelmed with my displeasing response to the God who not only saved my life, but also paid a tremendous price to do so. I want Him to change me. I want to please Him. I want to do things His way. I am very thankful for the next question in the scripture because, at least, I'm not left without the hope of a solution. I am very grateful that the prophet had the wherewithal to ask the question: In what way have I robbed you?   All of us should be sitting on the edge of our seat in anticipation of the answer to that question.   It is heart breaking that we even have to ask. God, who has literally given everything, not even withholding his very own son, and yet I have robbed him. In light of this truth I find myself broken, begging God for the answer. And then the response comes...

MALACHI 3:9-10 (NKJV) – "You are cursed with a curse, for you have robbed Me, *Even* this whole nation. [10] Bring all the tithes into the storehouse, that there may be food in My house, and try Me now in this," says the Lord

> of hosts, "if I will not open for you the windows of heaven and pour out for you *such* blessing that *there will* not *be room* enough *to receive it.*"

This section of scripture is so necessary and important for us to understand. I stated earlier that the world could be changed through a sacrificial Christ following church, but the question that is still in front of us is how? As we continue through this chapter, you will begin to see an unfolding of the power for change that is contained within the church. The power of the church is made plain in this section of scripture: tithes and offerings. The tithe is 10% of each person's income and the offering is anything over that. These tithes and offerings are brought into the storehouse.

We must consider, for a moment, what God is saying. God is requiring of every believer that they tithe 10% of their income or they are robbing God. However, if you read this more carefully, it really reads that God is requiring that the believers give an offering over his 10% or they are robbing God. That is what the scripture says. God has a powerful giving idea and it is called the church. When we are not obedient to what he is asking us to give, we are robbing God. We can't avoid what this scripture is telling us. If we do, we are, in the most basic of terms, trying to justify our disobedience.

Let's examine it a bit further. Don't forget that God stop there. It is in the next sentence that His powerful message of world change is revealed. God begins by telling us that we are living under a curse. As a matter of fact, the whole nation is under a curse when we are not obeying God. Let us remember where we started. If God does not change then what we read here must be seen somewhere else in scripture, and it is. In Deuteronomy 28, we find in that if we obey God then we will be the head and not the tail, the lender and not the borrower, our cities, land, and lives will be blessed. It goes on to discuss that our enemies will be destroyed and the nations will see it. The chapter does not finish there. It goes on to talk about the consequences of disobedience and they all begin with the word, "cursed." As the American church, we have the propensity to believe that we could never be cursed; but, we can. Later in Malachi, he goes on to say that the cursing comes from the devourer. From the canon of scripture, we know the devourer is Satan.

Up to this point, we see that in Malachi 3 the prophet is making a simple blessing and cursing equation. When the people of God are obedient to give tithes and offerings, the blessings of God comes upon them. When they walk in disobedience, they walk with the devourer.

Now you may be thinking, like many others I have spoken

to through the years, I don't tithe and I have plenty for new cars, new houses, and whatever else I want. But what they don't realize is that the devourer is not just after your finances. These same people have kids who are not serving the Lord, and all I can see is that the devourer has consumed parts of their life because of disobedience and they don't even realize it.

The intention of this booklet is not to be harsh but, in fact, my heart is for you and your family that you may prosper in the Lord. How can we learn if no one will teach us? My heart is to teach you true blessing and true cursing. If we are never told the truth about giving than there is a greater chance that we are living in the shadow of the devourer. It is through mercy that I want to show you the way out.

The next portion talks about bringing all of the tithes into the storehouse. You may be asking what is the storehouse? This term was used for the place where the Israelites brought their tithes and offerings to the priests. It was all stored in the storehouse. The bible doesn't give a clear understanding on what the storehouse was; however, we can draw some logical conclusions. It was local. It was for the Levites of that area. So, it would seem that the logical comparison to our modern time would be bringing all of the tithes and offerings into the local church.

It is a sad reality that in this day and age many people feel they cannot trust their local pastor with their tithes and offerings. There are some very clear discrepancies in this line of thinking. Either you are being spiritually fed by someone that you can't trust or you are deceiving yourself into believing that you don't need to give to your local church. There are so many pastors that are working with minimal salaries because that is seen as holy or chaste. I am not implying that pastors should be paid exorbitant salaries, but I do believe that they should be some of the best paid people in the church. The weight that they carry is tremendous, and all too often they carry it alone. They are subject to unrelenting spiritual attacks on them and their families. There is so much pressure that is placed on them. The last thing they should have to worry about is finances.

MALACHI 3:10B-11 — "Bring all the tithes into the storehouse, that there may be food in My house, and try Me now in this,' says the LORD of hosts, 'If I will not open for you the windows of heaven and pour out for you *such* blessing that *there will* not *be room* enough *to receive it*. 'And I will rebuke the devourer for your sakes, so that he will not destroy the fruit of your ground, nor shall the vine fail to bear fruit for you in the field,' says the LORD of hosts;"

What an astounding thought! God, Himself, says that if you give these tithes and offerings He is going to open the windows of heaven for you! He goes on to say that He is going to pour out such a blessing that you can't even contain it. The most amazing statement is when He tells us to test Him in this! He is ready and willing for you to test Him on the truthfulness of this statement. It is one of the only places in the Bible that we are given this opportunity. God never does anything without intention. He has a plan and he wants us to be a part of that plan. He knows and sees things that we have not even thought of yet; but, first, we need to cover some truths about the devourer. It says that God will rebuke the devourer. If that is the case, then who do you think is blinding your eyes so that you do not know the truth about the giving of your tithes and offerings? The devourer, of course! He whispers in your ear that tithing is just law; tithing is not in the New Testament; you should only tithe if your heart is right and cheerful; if you tithe you are not going to be able to pay your bills. These are lies. Lies that we believe. Lies that are robbing us of God's blessings. God, Himself, told us to test Him in this.

It is a sad reality, as we mentioned before, that certain televangelists and pastors have both polluted and diluted the message of tithing. The devourer has done a good job deceiving many. However, the word of God is living, powerful and active. The enemy knows what will happen if the power of a giving church is realized. Through these last few verses, we will see the impact of that church.

> MALACHI 3:12 – "And all nations will call you blessed, for you will be a delightful land," says the LORD of hosts."

The nations will call us blessed and call us a delightful land? Wait a minute? How does this happen? I believe that we, as Americans, live in the greatest country in the world. I have traveled to many parts of the world. I have seen poverty, orphans, hunger, and a great deficit of the basic human necessities. There is an overall lack of health and health care. It is heartbreaking. It is tragic. It is ours to solve and, really, it is not that difficult. How can the nations call us blessed if they have never seen us do anything to help them? The poor in other countries are incapable of even seeing or knowing what we have. They don't have TVs, the Internet, or other sources of news; and, even if they could afford it, they don't have time to sit around watching a program. They are too busy gathering food, cooking, and getting up the next day to do the very same thing. So, how can anything change? There is this light, this mighty beacon, and it is called the believers of the Most High God. We believe in this Bible we have. We believe in the God whom we serve. We walk in obedience to His Word.

What if every Christian church in the United States gave tithes and offerings? What if we obeyed His Word? Think about it for a moment: There are approximately 400,000 churches in our country alone. If every believer followed this simple Scripture and gave tithes and offerings as God says we should, this would equal billions and billions of dollars. This simple change in mindset and obedience is the key to solving problems in our community, our nation, and ultimately the world. We would have the resources to go into places like Uganda and solve the water crisis. We could go into Sudan and secure safe homes for every orphan. We could give a salary to the local music teacher who had her job cut. We could put up playgrounds and give single parents the assistance they need. We would proclaim with our actions that Christianity is the answer and Jesus is real. Through our communal obedience, we could have the resources that we need to care for the widows and orphans and so many more.

The enemy knows the power that our unity and obedience will bring. He has put all of his minions on high alert. He must fight this truth and keep it from as many believers as he can. He is fighting right now as you try to read this book. It is time to rise up and begin to live this biblical truth and release the world changing power that it holds. We have to begin to weigh whether a new couch is worth more than the life of an orphan. How many souls are on the other side of your obedience? Imagine the power of Islam being broken because the Christian church is doing what they are called to do. They are solving the world's problems and doing it through God's simple plan of tithes and offerings. The world doesn't have a poverty problem. It has a Christian giving problem.

Can you see it? The answer to the world's problems lies right in the center of the church of the Most High God. His plan is clear, simple, and achievable. The matter of obedience in tithes and offerings is God's plan to show the world the greatness of a nation founded on Him and showing Jesus to a lost and dying world. As the church, let us take on this challenge of obedience. If you are giving tithes, that is great, but we must remember that the Bible speaks of tithes and offerings. If you are not tithing, can you see what God's eternal plan is and join His mighty army? Can you give yourselves to *obedience* and, by doing so, allow the rest of the world to see a nation that is truly blessed and does not live for itself only? The world awaits our obedience.

Let's consider a few other thoughts on tithes and offerings so that we can solidify the point... It is that important!

THE PROMISE
OF GOD'S BLESSING

There are few subjects in the Christian church that are as sensitive and controversial as tithing. Tithing is a time-honored practice of giving the first 10 percent of our income to the Lord and his work. The word tithe means, "a tenth." The Scriptures mention tithing 40 times, in several different places, in both the Old and New Testament. Some translations of the Bible do use the word tenth instead of the word tithe, but the principle is the same. It is interesting to note that it was 40 years that God tested his people, the Israelites, in the desert. We believe that God tests the depth of our obedience and devotion to Him by the way that we use the finances and resources that He has entrusted to us. God promises a blessing to those who give tithes and offerings. The second part of that promise is a curse to those who rob Him.

These promises are powerful, both for the positive and the negative. As we talked about in the beginning of this booklet, God, who does not change, put theses strong words in the very last book of the Old Testament. It must, therefore, be important for us to find out what God desires and expects of us in our giving.

CHURCHES
JUST WANT
OUR MONEY

As a pastor, it is not easy for me to bring up the subject of money in a sermon. This difficulty is highlighted even more when you bring up the doctrine that believers have to give. Over the last twenty or thirty years, the Christian church in America has received a lot of negative attention because the shady financial dealings of some ministers and the daily appeals for financial donations to support radio and television ministries. This has made it much more difficult for ministers to proclaim the whole counsel of God (Acts 20:27) when the "whole counsel of God" includes the subject of faithful financial giving by God's people. It is hard, as a pastor, to bring up this subject without it sounding like it is a conflict of interests. I, after all, live and support my family through the faithful giving of people in the local church. Unlike the secular business world though, I am compelled by the truth of the Bible to preach about tithing as one of the Lord's messengers. I believe that I must carefully spell out what I believe God asks of all of us in the area of giving. We all want to be obedient, close the mouth of the devourer, and experience the blessing of the Lord through faithful financial giving.

THAT IS OLD TESTAMENT!

One of the first objections people raise when someone brings up the subject of tithing is this, tithing is Old Testament teaching and we are not under the law anymore. This argument against tithing does not, however, hold up. There is evidence that God's people paid tithes before God gave the law, which had specific instructions on tithing.

- Abraham paid tithes to Melchizedek, priest of the Most High God. This was after God had given Abraham a great victory. See Genesis 14:18-20 and Hebrews 7:5-9

- Jacob, who was in exile, vowed to give God a tenth of all God had given him, if God would be with him and bring him safely back to his father's house. See Genesis 28:18-22

In Deuteronomy 26:12-13, God makes tithing the law in Israel. The tithe that is brought into the storehouse is to be given to the Levites (God's ministers in the sanctuary), the stranger, the fatherless, and the widow. In other words, the tithe ultimately went to *people* (for further study please see Leviticus 27:30-32; Numbers 18:24-28; Deuteronomy 12:6-17, 14:22-28; Nehemiah 10:37-38, 13:5,12)

It is interesting to note that Jesus specifically referred to the tithe when He confronted the Pharisees, who, were experts in precise tithing. These Pharisees were zealous to tithe on everything that they got; but, they had neglected the more important matters of the heart (justice, mercy, faith and love of God). Jesus did not do away with their tithing but called them to deal with the matters of the heart *also*. (see Matthew 23:23; Luke 11:42)

We can see through these verses that tithing is not just mentioned in the law of Moses, but it is, in fact, a doctrine that it prolific through the entirety of the scriptures. God speaks of it in the beginning before the law in Genesis, during the restoration period in Nehemiah, in the prophetic books in Malachi, in the gospels of Matthew and Luke, and finally it is mentioned in the book of Hebrews. It is one of the rare times that we see a doctrine mentioned in all five aspects of scripture.

WE ARE
UNDER GRACE

When tithing is introduced into the conversation, people often counter with the argument that we are under grace, not under the law. Under grace, it all belongs to God. However, when this point is made, my mind returns to the argument that was made in the previous section. The doctrine of tithing took place outside of the time and dispensation of the law of Moses. I have no desire to put anybody under a burden of legalistic giving. Giving is a reflection of your heart. Ask yourself why you are not giving. If you use the argument that under grace it is all God's money, then why don't you share it with Him? OR Do you just use this argument to simply appease your conscience for giving little or nothing to your local church? Some have said that if it is all God's money under grace then what is the big deal about giving him 10% in return? I would agree with this statement. It is not only the 10 percent that belongs to God (though He does require it) but, if we are being honest, our tithe, our offering, and ultimately everything we have belongs to Him.

IS IT STILL POSSIBLE TO ROB GOD?

Could it be that we are asking the wrong question? The focus of this section is not about tithing for the Christian; but rather, asking if we can rob God in the age of grace. God tells us in Malachi 3:6 that He does not change and then challenges His people to turn back to Him. How were they to turn back to Him? They turned back to Him by bringing into His storehouse all the tithes and offerings. Their failure to give God their tithes and offerings was theft, according to God.

> PROVERBS 3:9-10 – "Honor the Lord with your possessions, and with the first fruits of **all** your increase; so your barns will be filled with plenty, and your vats will overflow with new wine." *(emphasis added)*

Israel was an agricultural nation whose wealth was invested in livestock and crops. A good yield in crops and healthy livestock was a sign of prosperity and blessing from God. This will be important to understand as you keep reading. It is true that we are no longer under the law of Moses; but, the law of sowing and reaping is very much in effect today (Galatians 6:6-10). The law of sowing and reaping is a cause and effect relationship that is vital to understand. It is this relationship that illustrates for us what is going to happen when we give or do not give. Much like gravity, the law of sowing and reaping is always at work in our lives whether we see it or not.

One of the saddest things to hear are the excuses that prosperous American believers give for not obeying God in the area of giving. We are the most prosperous nations on earth! When we do not give, we rob God. This, in turn, robs us of the blessing that is promised us when we obey. We *will* reap what we sow. If you do not give to God, there is a sad truth, and if you are a faithful giver, there is a wonderful truth, we will reap what we sow for all eternity. This is a sober truth, yet it *is* truth. Many people have said that they can't afford to tithe. The honest truth, however, is that as a Christian you can't afford not to tithe. The Bible is clear in calling our tithe the first fruit. In other words, it should be our first act of obedience when it comes to our finances. This act of obedience is saying God, we love you and trust you. We are showing God that we want to give Him our first and best. Out of this heart, tithing becomes relationship-oriented rather than law-demanded. Jesus said that we are his friends if we do what He commands. Our relationship is established through obedience, even obedience to tithe. The whole thought of financial blessing begins scripturally with the tithe. So, if we want God's blessing we cannot afford not to tithe.

DID THE DEVOURER DIE 2000 YEARS AGO OR IS HE STILL ALIVE AND WELL?

God promised in Malachi 3:11 that He would rebuke the Devourer for His people if they were faithful to bring their tithes and offerings into the storehouse (the local church). Who or what was this Devourer that God promised to rebuke? Was it a demon? Satan? A natural calamity? The Devourer is not clearly identified; however, *his* work *is*. We see a clear example of the work of this devourer in Deuteronomy when he devoured all of the Israelites, crops because of their disobedience. God promised abundant blessing in Deuteronomy 28:1-14, if his people would obey Him diligently. He also promised that curses against them would be multiplied if they were disobedient (Deuteronomy 28:15-68). There was a time in Israel's history after the Babylonian captivity that the Devourer had a field day with the people of God. God had brought His people back to their homeland to rebuild the city of Jerusalem and the temple which had been ransacked by the Babylonian army. Unfortunately, the people began thinking about their own welfare, prosperity, and safety. They became consumed with rebuilding *their* individual homes while the house of God lay in waste. As a result, their crops failed; their clothing did not keep them warm; their money burned holes in their pockets; and there was a drought in the land. All of this happened because they put their own material interests ahead of God's house (see Haggai 1:1-11).

I have watched God rebuke the Devourer many times over the years. So many times I have seen God make the material possessions of His faithful givers last longer. He blesses them with financial bargains. He blesses them with longer lasting cars, appliances, shoes, etc. Virtually every area of a giver's life is touched with the blessing of God. On the other hand, I have also watched with sadness some people who do not give God their tithes and offerings, struggle with their finances Their vehicles frequently break down. They are often plagued with numerous, costly, visits to the doctor's office. They end up paying top dollar prices for things. They have family problems. The list goes on and on. We need to learn quickly about God's blessings and learn to be faithful. Yes, it is true that God will sometimes test you with times of deprivation and other forms of adversity, just as he did with Job. We need to ask ourselves how faithful we have been to God when adversity comes our way. It may be more than a test. It may be the Devourer eating up our precious resources. If that is the case, we need to repent and return in obedience to the word of God.

IS IT A SIN FOR A MINISTER TO LIVE WELL?

There is a well-known proverb that you may have heard about being as poor as a church mouse. A really poor individual is sometimes said to be as poor as a church mouse. This saying has been perpetuated by a common belief among God's people that His ministers should subsist on the bare necessities. It is true that a minister is commanded to work unto the Lord a single heart, not looking to the ministry as a lucrative racket. This raises the question though, is it right for God's people to expect their ministers and missionaries to just get by? A minister is given the eternal responsibility to look out for the souls of their sheep (Hebrews 13:17) and we want them to be worried about finances as well? The children of many of God's ministers grow up despising the ministry and sometimes even turning away from the Lord, in part, because of what their parents go through and give up for God's people. Imagine what many pastors' children see. They watch their parents under tremendous pressure and yet they can't, in many cases, even afford some little luxuries in life. Luxuries such as going out for dinner or a scoop of ice cream or even a much needed family vacation. Scriptures exhort us to look after our leaders who feed us the word of God. Elders (i.e., pastors) who labor in the Word and teaching are said to be worthy of double honor (this is historically used as a financial term, not just meaning respect) for their work.

(1 Timothy 5:17-18)

I have often been saddened and amazed at what I see in some churches, in which church leaders are asked to live on paltry salaries. It doesn't make any sense to me. These are the very leaders to whom we trust our spiritual lives, the most important area of our lives! Yet, in many cases, executives and business owners that attend that same church can make exorbitantly more money and we would never question or even think that was wrong. We would consider the successful and wealthy businessman in the congregation as blessed. Should we not hold the same standard regarding the ministry? I am of the firm conviction that pastors, not all but most, throughout the U.S. are some of the lowest paid professionals in our country. As the scripture declares, brethren, these things ought not to be so.

It is important to note that the obedience in your giving (tithes and offerings) directly affects the salaries that are paid to pastors, assistants, youth pastors, etc. In other words, salaries obviously are *only and can only* be based upon what comes in from the tithes and offerings. Therefore, each individual family and their faithfulness absolutely and directly affects your church staff's salaries. So, suddenly your obedience is not only connected to your own family but it is connected to loving the other families in your church as well. A loving flock takes care of its leaders making sure their financial lives are the least, and I mean *least*, thing they concern themselves with.

GOD LOVES A CHEERFUL GIVER

In the early church it was common for the believers to help each other financially. In the early days, a person who became a Christian often lost their homes, their jobs and their inheritance. On one particular occasion, Paul let the believers in Corinth know of the need to help other Christians that had become impoverished. *Paul asked for money.* He encouraged them to give, generously (sow bountifully) because God loves a cheerful (literally, hilarious) giver. God does not want us to give grudgingly or against our will. He wants us to experience the joy that comes when we open ourselves up to the needs around us and give ourselves away (See 2 Corinthians 9:1-13). This is an interesting look into who God loves; He loves a cheerful giver. If you want to experience the love of God in a greater way; perhaps this is a wonderful key for you. It is abundantly clear that giving with a cheerful heart will catch the attention of God's love.

We also need to point out that it is not Biblically wrong to raise money for worthwhile causes. King Solomon and Moses raised money for the building of the temple and the sanctuary (Exodus 25:1-9; 1 Chronicles 29:1-9). We should give offerings like this as the Lord leads. We should not automatically question the motives of those who seek to raise money; we should trust that the Lord is going to lead us to where He would like us to give. It is a good thing to invest in the kingdom of God. The work of the Kingdom requires money, and God has chosen us to be a part of His incredible plan to change the world.

IS JESUS THE LORD OF YOUR MONEY?

The matter of giving back to God from what He has given us is really a matter of the Lordship of Jesus Christ in our lives. There are many people who want Jesus to save them from the penalty of their sins, but they get very upset when told they must surrender their lives in obedience to His rule. This gets very practical when it comes to the life of a Christian. The Bible tells us that the earth is the Lord's and the fullness thereof (Psalm 24:1). The truth of the matter is that our very lives, to say nothing of our money and our possessions, all belong to the Lord Jesus Christ. So we must ask ourselves, am I willing to open up my heart to this critical area of faithfulness with money? It is through this faithfulness that He will, not only lead your life, but He will use you to change the world. The kingdom of God takes finances. May it be said that we have loved the Lord even down to our finances.

One of the most powerful scriptures about how we handle our money can be found in:

LUKE 19:11-27 — Now as they heard these things, He spoke another parable, because He was near Jerusalem and because they thought the kingdom of God would appear immediately. Therefore, He said: "A certain nobleman went into a far country to receive for himself a kingdom and to return. So he called ten of his servants, delivered to them ten minas, and said to them, 'Do business till I come.' But his citizens hated him, and sent a delegation after him, saying, 'We will not have this *man* to reign over us.'

"And so it was that when he returned, having received the kingdom, he then commanded these servants, to whom he had given the money, to be called to him, that he might know how much every man had gained by trading. Then came the first, saying, 'Master, your mina has earned ten minas.' And he said to him, 'Well *done*, good servant; because you were faithful in a very little, have authority over ten cities.' And the second came, saying, 'Master, your mina has earned five minas.' Likewise, he said to him, 'You also be over five cities.'

"Then another came, saying, 'Master, here is your mina, which I have kept put away in a handkerchief. For I feared you, because you are an austere man. You collect what you did not deposit, and reap what you did not sow.' And he said to him, 'Out of your own mouth I will judge you, *you* wicked servant. You knew that I was an austere man, collecting what I did not deposit and reaping what I did not sow. Why then did you not put my money in the bank, that at my coming I might have collected it with interest?'

"And he said to those who stood by, 'Take the mina from him, and give *it* to him who has ten minas.' (But they said to him, 'Master, he has ten minas.') 'For I say to you, that to everyone who has will be given; and from him who does not have, even what he has will be taken away from him. But bring here those enemies of mine, who did not want me to reign over them, and slay *them* before me.'"

As you carefully read this, you will begin to see that this promise, perhaps, supersedes all other promises in the New Testament (outside of eternal life, of course). What is Jesus saying here? If you are faithful with little; you will be faithful with much. This verse is specifically in regard to money. Jesus often talked about money and giving. In fact, some scholars say that Jesus talked about money more than any other truth. Jesus knows that where our treasure is, there our heart will be. Our heart follows our treasure not the other way around. If we are faithful with how we handle our finances, God will give us cities as our reward. What?! Jesus said He will give us cities if we are simply faithful with a little. It was His idea!

I once talked to a man who had been given a substantial amount of money. He was somewhat bemoaning the fact that he could have used the monies for his own purposes and that maybe he should have. I brought the above verse up to him and honestly asked, "Why would you trade a city for a house, or a boat or anything else? That seems like a bad investment." This man left our conversation with a better perspective and outlook on life. So how about you? Will you settle for mere "things?" or do you want to be faithful with the things that God has given you and plant seeds and inherit cities? The answer seems obvious to me. The whole crux of the parable rests on this; we will not have this *man* to reign over us. So who gets to reign over your finances? Who is the Lord of your finances? King Jesus? Or you? How you handle your money will determine how much God entrusts you with. That is powerful and exciting! We get the amazing opportunity to join forces with Him, the Creator of all things.

WHAT DO WE TEACH OUR CHILDREN?

Of all the areas in life that are important to me, the most important is what I teach my children. I think about transferring truth to my children in every aspect of life. What do I teach them about Jesus? What do I teach them about others in the world? Is math truly important? In fact, I find it interesting when I hear parents say that the most important thing they want to teach their children is to follow their hearts. They don't think that obedience is as important as following your heart. Some parents use this argument in regard: to church life, worship, school, family life, and many other areas. Can we take a minute and at least think that through? What if your child came home and said I have decided that I'm not going to do math anymore, it's just not in my heart? Our parental response would, hopefully, be swift and to the point: You are going to do math, in fact, you are going to do it well or you are grounded until you are 22 (said with humor).

So, I have to ask the question. How much more important are we to teach them the things of God? How much more important are: worship, giving, serving, and the other things of the Kingdom? I think they trump math, english, and science every single day of the week. I am not saying that these subjects are not important, they are. I am saying that the Kingdom of God and His ways are eternal; thus, we need to be teaching our children about all of His ways.

What do we teach them about giving, obedience to God's Word, and helping others? Do we teach them that tithes and offerings are critical? Do we teach them that helping our community means more than just giving them *material things*? Do we share age appropriate information with them about the tough, hard, truth of what the rest of the world is like or do we only paint a picture of the American dream and what that looks like? Do you take them on mission trips? Do you let them view pictures and movies about other's lives throughout the world, even when it brings tears or discomfort?

What would they say about the things that you, as their parents, have modeled to them? If asked, how would they describe your giving? Would they say you are extravagant givers?

World changing givers? Or takers? What would they say is they were asked: What would the church look like if everyone was like their Mom or Dad? Think about it. What do your children see in everything from your church attendance, your serving of others, and your giving? It's important!

One of the greatest issues we face today is the entitled American. We must confront it. God is watching! We must teach our children that the reason we have a privileged lifestyle is so that God can use all of us and our finances to grow the Kingdom of God! Their eternity depends on it; And, quite frankly, so does yours. I'm not talking about whether we go to heaven or hell; but, I am talking about God's eternal rewards and the responsibility we take on when we choose to teach others what God wants them to know or choose not to teach them what God wants them to know. I know this is heavy, but please think it through. Ask God to show you where you are doing well and where you need improvement. Ask Him if you are teaching your children the value of giving? It just may be that you are raising up a future Mother Theresa, ora Billy Graham, or a kingdom business owner. It just may be that you are raising up future missionaries, pastors, leaders in the kingdom. It just may be that you are raising up future millionaires and financial changers of the world. At the very least, we are teaching our children to be Christians who can change the world with their obedience. Let's make sure we do it in the power of the Word and His Holy Spirit. I will be praying for you as you undertake this very crucial mission!

THE SEEDS OF MALACHI 3

There is a point in Malachi 3, that is missed or often, not even thought of. I believe that every Israelite would have understood this point. They were primarily a farming economy. They would understand that we give 10 percent to the Lord, we give, let's say, another 10 percent for offering, and we have 80 percent left. Now, let's say that you use the other 80 percent to pay bills, etc., then we have a real problem! There would be no seed for the following year and thus no harvest. They would have starved to death. They knew a key piece of information that may help and challenge us in our lives. So, let us consider the *seed*.

I want to remind all of us what the Bible says in Deuteronomy 28. We are called to be the head and not the tail and the lender and not the borrower. In all honesty, we have to say that we are neither of those things. In the world today we are taught to spend, spend, spend. With this as our financial framework, we are going to be working our whole lives and yet the world still owns us through our debt. So, what is the problem? I think that we keep giving away our *seed*. If we are tithing 10 percent and we are giving an offering as God leads us, we are still left with a large portion of our income. What if we took another 10 percent of our income and invest it? We are going to take our *seed* and we are going to save it because we *have* to prepare for coming harvests. I truly believe that this is God's plan for the believer. There is one other concept that we must fully embrace for this *seed* method to take shape. That is a four letter word called work.

Now, let me blow your mind a little. What is considered the biblical work week? God, Himself, worked for six days. Jesus said that there are twelve hours in the day for work. I think that the Devil has blinded us by making us focus on a 40-hour work week. I am all for spending more time with your families and I think that is vitally important. I also believe that a 40-hour work week is robbing us of an incredible life giving answer. God's idea was to work extra hours to get a blessing that will change the world. What if you work your 40-hour job and then take a part time job working 10-15 hours a week? Then, we took that *seed* and invested it. Let's do the math. If you worked 15 hours per week for $10 an hour (which is a very conservative number) that is roughly $8,000 per year. You do this for just five years. After 30 years at only 8%, you would have $420,000! Do you see what the enemy is robbing from us? A *little* extra work and we'd be the head and not the tail, the lender and not the borrower. We can teach this principle to our children, the church, and other people. We can show them how to save their *seed* too.

We, as Christians, should also be thinking generationally. What if every church did something for the next generation? Let's say they buy a house, pay it off and then give it to the next generation to use. Then they give it to the next generation to use. There are around 400,000 churches in the U.S. alone. Let's say that the average house is $125,000. Do you know how much money that would be in the Kingdom? That is 5 billion dollars and that is only on one investment. The possibilities are endless.

HOLY BUSINESS

Does God perform miracles in business? Is He concerned about the mountains we face in our workplace? Yes! God wants to be involved in every aspect of our lives.

> MATTHEW 17:20 – He replied, "Because you have so little faith, I tell you the truth, if you have faith as small as a mustard seed, you can say to this mountain, 'move from here to there' and it will move, nothing will be impossible for you."

Gunnar Olson, the Swedish founder of the International Christian Chamber of Commerce, tells a story about a miracle in his own business. He owns a plastics company in Sweden. They make huge plastic bags that cover bales of hay. When it was harvest season, they made an alarming discovery. In the more than 1,000 pallets of those bags that were ready for shipment, every bag on the warehouse floor had been sealed shut from top to bottom.

Scientists declared the entire stock worthless trash. There was nothing they could do. The company would go out of business. Gunnar and his family sought the Lord in prayer, and the Holy Spirit spoke through various family members. One said, if God can turn water into wine, what are plastics to Him? Another felt the circumstance was not from the Lord and that they should stand against it. So, they took authority and began to pray, laying hands on every pallet and asking the Lord to restore the bags to a suitable condition. As you can imagine, this took several hours! Upon inspecting the bags, they discovered that every single bag had been restored. An incredible miracle had taken place!

At times, the Lord will have you walk a special journey within your own journey. You might be on a path advancing His cause when He begins to lead you in a unique direction. I'm always amazed to note how often God performs unbelievable acts in our lives, even though we might not be aware of them until much later.

Have you ever been in a trial and wondered, *what in the world is happening?* It is only afterward that it become clear. God has moved with many of our church businesses in the same way. I can't take any credit for what I write here. It was all God's doing, one miracle after another and one provision after another. God not only showed that He is *Jehovah-Jireh*, the Lord our provider; but that He is still the same God of miracles who walked the earth 2,000 years ago. He is the same yesterday, today, and forever.

The next part of the story picks up as I was finishing Bible school in 1988. While there, my wife and I had sold everything we had, including our house, and spent all of our savings. Our time there was great and God used it significantly by giving us much needed instruction; but, we returned to Michigan without a dime in our pockets and no back up plan. We owned one car.

I was offered a position as an assistant pastor with a $100 per week salary that included a small one-bedroom apartment. It was all the church congregation could offer, but we knew it was the Lord's will for me to take the position. With two children and a third on the way, money and living space were, understandably, at a premium. To express it as simply and as profoundly as I can, I thought, *I need to make more money!*

With my background in construction, I thought I could bid jobs and subcontract the labor. In other words, I could oversee the construction but still have time for church work. With that goal in mind, I founded a company called Gilchrist Construction (it took long hours to come up with that name!). We printed business cards and began looking for work.

At that time, a nursing home supervisor who attended our church told me about a home that was accepting bids on a huge roofing job. I turned in a quote. To my surprise, the quote I submitted was turned down. I called the vice president (who later became a good friend) and asked him if there was a problem with the bid. He informed that it was too low. Can you believe that? The bid was too low. He said, "You come with high recommendations, and I trust them; but, unless you raise your price by $10,000, we can't give you the work."

So, I raised the price and witnessed what turned out to be only the beginning of the miracles God had in store for that business. From that time forward, that vice president contracted Gilchrist Construction for every part of a $15 million dollar Greater Detroit nursing home renovation project. Our company hired contractors from within the church and paid them to remodel the nursing homes. It was astonishing. God set a plan in my heart back then that is still there today. I am convinced God wants to use us in far greater measures in this area of church business.

The ideas I share in this chapter are vital if you seek the blessing of God on your church businesses, I'm convinced of this. I'm not saying that churches can't prosper in other ways but, rather, that God is looking for something specific in church businesses.

For example, in the middle of the nursing home

renovation, God showed me clearly that He wanted me to give the profits to His Kingdom. It was simply a matter of obedience, and to be honest, it wasn't difficult. I'll explain why. Many years before, the Lord had asked me during a time of prayer, "which is more important to you? Your relationship with Me or your duty to Me?" I answered, "My relationship with You is most important, Lord." He then said something that shook me and has shaped my life ever since: "Your tithe is your duty and your offering is your relationship."

Let me ask you the same question the Lord asked me that day: Which is more important to you? I knew what God wanted from me; my offerings were to exceed my tithes. Now, I'm not saying this to put that expectation on any reader. God will test you with finances at His time and in His own unique way.

Deuteronomy 8 teaches that God sends His people into the wilderness to test them and to know their hearts, just as He did with Israel. At the time that God spoke to us about our giving, we didn't have two nickels to rub together. This was long before the remodeling project. God needed to know our hearts before He could entrust us. We didn't have any extra cash, but God wanted to reveal His names to us. He doesn't show Himself as Jehovah-Jireh, the Lord your Provider, when you have millions of dollars flowing through your hands. He shows you when you have pennies. He tests your heart to see what you will do with the pennies. Then, He will trust you with nickels, dimes, dollars, hundreds of dollars, and even thousands. He does it one step at a time.

I laugh when Christians say how great it would be to win the lottery (I'm not even going to address the ethics of Christians playing the lottery). I ask them what they would do with the money. They usually tell me that they would give the first 10% to the church as though that was admirable! God wants to pour money through your hands, but He can only do so if your hands are open. All your hypothetical lottery winnings belong to the Kingdom, not just 10%. God is testing you. Will you pass the test of being a Kingdom lover and, therefore, a Kingdom giver?

As we gave the profits away, the business grew, and the Lord opened other doors for us to walk through. While lamenting with two other pastors about the accusation that the church is always *asking* for money, we came up with an idea. Why not start companies that *give* money? We decided to establish a company called Shepherd Industries. While pumping gas one particularly frigid day, I came up with the idea to manufacture and market a piece of Velcro to wrap around itself for holding the gas handle open while pumping gas. Immediately, we ran with the idea and gas stations began selling them. The item was originally called the "Frustration Eliminator." In hindsight, that was a goofy name!

It was suggested that this wrap actually had thousands of other uses, such as wrapping extension cords and sleeping bags. We renamed it "Get-A-Grip™" and offered it to hardware stores. It really took off! In addition, K-Mart began carrying our product. It was a great seller. In fact, it was so great that the Velcro Corporation contacted us and made us a wonderful offer. If we would continue packaging this product, they would add it to their product line. We developed a good business relationship. As a matter of fact, the president of Velcro Corporation remains a good friend to this day.

One little idea has translated into sales of millions of units. Get-A-Grip™ still exists and continues to sell today. We have moved Shepherd Industries from Michigan to Northern New York, where it has provided jobs for many people. I tell this story because God had a big plan for us, just as He does for you. He is not finished. It is just beginning. Open up your mind, your heart, and your hands. We serve the creative God of the universe. There are many more ideas and plans to consider. Understand this: It will take hard work, but what a ride!

Remember, when we moved to New York, the great accusation of the Enemy was that *nothing would work*. The employment market was stagnant and people had stopped dreaming; but, God wanted to destroy the lies, defeat the mentality, and restore dreams once more. In fact, I believe it delights God to come into an area and show what He can do with obedient people.

It was clear that the area needed jobs. We already had one company, Shepherd Industries, providing work but God had more in mind. Tom, a good friend from Michigan, decided to move to New York to help with the church. Tom has a background in CAD (Computer Aided Drafting) and CAFM (Computer Aided Facilities Management). These skills are highly sought after in any job market.

During his first year here, Tom endured a two-hour commute to a vocational/technical school located in the next county where he had accepted a position as a CAD instructor. Do you think God may have been testing his heart? I believe so. Though Tom's students received first place in a statewide skills competition, Tom was unable to continue in his position because he was not certified to teach in New York State. Looking down the road, however, these apparent obstacles were all part of God's bigger plan, which was leading up to a miracle. My thought was, *let's start a business with Tom's skills*. CFS (CAD and Facilities

Services) was literally an overnight success, not because of our ideas or skills, but because we serve a God of miracles.

On one occasion, Tom and I traveled downstate to deliver a proposal to sell software for one of the world's largest CAFM companies. The president commented that he was unable to keep people in his drawing services division. The company hired and trained employees, but because of the high cost of living in a large metropolitan area, the employees soon left for better paying jobs with other companies.

Immediately, the wheels began turning in my head. Northern New York was not a large tech-driven area. We could hire people, pay them a fair wage, and keep them. Unable to contain myself, I blurted out that WE would be his drawing services division. Sometimes, the very aspects we view as disadvantages create a niche that others don't have. It was *because* we were in the country that we could fill this need. We didn't need to be big city people to see God's big plan.

Remember, at this time, Tom **was** the company! After a few moments of discussion, the president said yes. Hire four people tomorrow and let's see how this goes. It was a miracle! Today, CFS has fifteen full-time employees who make more money than most of the people in the county.

The company continues to play a huge part in providing valuable services and jobs to Northern New York.

Can you see God in all of this? The mentality was that nothing good could happen in our area. We, as God's people, showed the world that something powerful could happen. We showed people their dreams could come true as God used a Christian company to create jobs. Almighty God was reclaiming His ground. Just let that sink in!

We weren't finished, yet. I also started a construction business called MKG Homes. The timing of the Lord was truly awesome. This company was founded only months before the expansion of the local military base and a corresponding construction boom. We had no idea that demand would reach those levels when we started, but God knew, of course!

Settle this in your heart: Your Heavenly Father is looking down the road. He knows the future and is planning yours. He requires only your obedience to take you places you have never been. So, take your hands off of your finances and give them back to their rightful Owner. The money is not yours...it is His. He will bless and multiply all that you give Him.

I know of what I speak. I have given away the majority of

our business profits and I have personally witnessed God give more and more to fund His Kingdom. The realization has been overwhelming.

I have heard Christians of various ages say that it is boring to serve God. I present this argument. I came out of the drug world. I know what that is all about. There is no lasting excitement there. Everyone dresses the same, talks the same, and laughs at the same foolishness. It may be fun for a moment, but it is utterly boring and pointless after that.

As a Christian, however, I have been to most of the continents on our planet and have eaten the greatest food these exotic places have to offer. I have personally witnessed the events surrounding a military coup, complete with bombs exploding and bullets whizzing past me. I have been on safaris and whitewater rafting trips. I have piloted airplanes and flown in more planes than I can count. I have taught Sunday school classes with two people and preached to thousands under the same anointing. I have seen God channel millions of dollars through our hands. I'm telling you this...it's just the tip of the iceberg. Do you think any other way of life could really compare? It just can't. God is looking to do so much more. He is looking for you!

BUILDING A KINGDOM COMPANY

I want to show you how to build a kingdom company or, at least, give you some general guidelines. I can't emphasize enough that you call it a kingdom company and not hoard the profits for yourself and your desires. Don't deceive yourself by saying that when you give it all to your family you are really blessing the Kingdom. That is the voice of the Enemy. I am talking about a company that is totally dedicated to God: *That* is the essence of what I mean by a *kingdom company*.

I'm not saying secular companies can't work or that there is anything inherently wrong with them. They are just not the subject at hand. I am talking about a company owned and, therefore, blessed by the Lord Himself. Use this as a litmus test: What comes to mind when you think of *profit?* Is it a tangible, material thing like land, a new house, a car, or a board? If so, it's not His; the company, in that case, is yours.

Don't misunderstand me, I certainly believe in the abundant life and probably believe in prosperity more than most people. The phrase I prefer, however, is *abundant moderation.* By that I mean that it is all right to have a nice home and other material possessions that you enjoy. A life of abundance can reveal so much about the glory and goodness of God. The moderation part means that you don't need 15 bedrooms, 12 bathrooms, and a Mercedes for your dog. I am sure you get the point.

If you call it a kingdom company, you give the remaining profit to the Lord's work. It's really His anyway. God wants to rain riches upon His people, so we can share the blessing with others and not fill our own coffers. If you gave me a million dollars today, I could begin to take every disabled person off the streets of Nepal and put them in a Christian home where they would be loved and cared for. We could shine the light of the gospel on all those rejected by the Hindu caste system.

Don't be ashamed to think big about finances. God needs big givers. He is looking for people to start kingdom companies. The Scriptures is clear on this subject:

MATTHEW 6:31-33 — "Therefore, do not worry, saying, 'What shall we eat?' or 'What shall we drink?' or 'What shall we wear?' For after all these things the Gentiles seek. For your heavenly Father knows that you need all these things. But seek first the Kingdom of God and His righteousness, and all these things shall be added to you."

COLOSSIANS 3:23-24 – "In all you do, do it heartily, as to the Lord, and not unto men; knowing that from the Lord you will receive the reward of the inheritance: for you serve the Lord Christ."

We first dedicate our profit to the Lord. It is His. As you read, perhaps you already own a business and want to dedicate it or rededicate it to the Lord. Take the time to pray now. Reaffirm your commitment to Him.

WHAT DO YOU THINK ABOUT YOUR AREA?

Many Christians tend to think too small. Have you ever heard a pastor or a missionary describe the region in which they minister as a "tough place?" It is true that some areas are tougher than others but, don't be discouraged. We went into a rural area of New York with few jobs and saw a new business prosper because of God's Word.

We must change how we think about our areas and, specifically, about church and business. The Bible says:

> **2 CORINTHIANS 10:5** – "Casting down arguments and every high thing that exalts itself against the knowledge of God, bring every thought into captivity to the obedience of Christ."

> **PSALM 24:1** – "The earth is the Lord's, and all its fullness, the world and those who dwell therein."

The real issue is belief. Do you walk by faith or by sight?

In Luke 19, Jesus talks to the disciples about the Kingdom. They ask Him what they should do after He leaves. He didn't want them to wonder how to live. He didn't want them to contemplate hiding out in a cave. In the midst of His Kingdom discussion, Jesus tells them to *occupy* or *do business* until He comes. This is the command of the Lord. He tells us that the church should occupy until He comes. This is not just a theory; it is the Word of God. In fact, the phrase *"do business"* is not only a commercial mandate, it is an all-inclusive command to every believer about every aspect of life.

We have to think differently than we ever have before. The Bible tells us that we are the head and not the tail (Deuteronomy 28:13). Why should we be content to allow non-believers to own the businesses that control the job market? Though we want them blessed as well, shouldn't all profit from these businesses be given to the Kingdom of God? Consider what we could do with these finances. We have to start thinking big. For example, imagine if every church invested wisely to bless the next generation.

Using my own church as an example, think in terms of how these principles apply to your own church. Imagine if the generation before us had purchased a piece of property on the scenic St. Lawrence River with the intent to bless those in the generations to come. It might have been a sacrifice, but that investment, however little it cost them at the time, would be worth millions of dollars today!

Continue to imagine. We take that money and use it for the Kingdom today, and then do something bigger for the next generation. What if half of the churches in the United States did the same thing? Are you getting the picture? We would *already* have enough to feed our communities. We would have the best programs in the best facilities, all adequately funded. We could build home after home and orphanage upon orphanage on the mission field with one simple forward-looking notion. Imagine if we imparted this kind of thinking to every person in our churches. Wealth would abound! Kingdom wealth!

The Scripture is full of this kind of thinking. Abraham was wealthy. The tribes of Israel were wealthy. Moses was wealthy. David and Solomon were mega-millionaires.

Why do we think that holiness in prayer and worship is somehow amplified by poverty?

The book of James addresses this subject and tells us that useless religion is defined as merely telling the needy to be warm and filled. We, the church, are supposed to be the answer to their needs. Besides preaching, praying, and giving spiritual direction, Christian leadership, with these principles, can also provide income and jobs for people. Pastors can help their parishioners have a better life.

You read that right! Far from being limited to the spiritual side of life, shepherding should involve all aspects of life. I'm certainly not advocating that every pastor starts a company, but I am strongly suggesting that we open our hearts and lives to other things that God may want us to do. Jesus made an interesting statement to Peter:

> MATTHEW 16:18-19 — "And I also say to you that you are Peter, and on this rock I will build My church, and the gates of Hades shall not prevail against it. And I will give you the keys of the Kingdom of the heaven, and whatever you bind on earth will be bound in heaven, and whatever you loose on earth will be loosed in heaven."

What was Jesus saying? Gates are to keep things out. Gates are for defense, not offense. I have never had a gate attack me! I am sure you haven't either! We have to get this straight: Jesus said the church is to be so much on the offensive that the gates of hell will not be able to stop anything we do. So, our thinking must change. Hell cannot stop the church unless we let it. Nothing can stop the church. We must begin to claim that this area is ours. This county is ours. We are here to see the prosperity of the Lord. We are to pour over our walls into cities and communities so that the church can fulfill its calling. The church is a city on a hill with its light unhidden.

Look into the Christian life of the future. What do you see? Do you see a land of prosperity? Do you see the church being the focal point of all that goes on? Haggai asked the same thing. Read and meditate on it:

HAGGAI 2:1-9 — In the seventh month, on the twenty-first of the month, the word of the Lord came by Haggai the prophet, saying: "Speak now to Zerubbabel the son of Shealtiel, governor of Judah, and to Joshua the son of Jehozadak, the high priest, and to the remnant of the people, saying: 'Who is left among you who saw this temple in its former glory? And how do you see it now? In comparison with it, is this not in your eyes as nothing?' 'Yet now be strong, Zerubbabel,' says the Lord; 'and be strong, Joshua, son of Jehozadak, the high priest; and be strong, all you people of the land,' says the Lord, 'and work; for I am with you,' says the Lord of hosts. 'According to the word that I covenanted with you when you came out of Egypt, so My Spirit remains among you; do not fear!'" For thus says the Lord of hosts: 'Once more (it is a little while) I will shake heaven and earth, the sea and dry land; and I will shake all nations, and they shall come to the Desire of All Nations, and will fill this temple with glory,' says the Lord of hosts. 'The silver is Mine, and the gold is Mine,' says the Lord of hosts. 'The glory of this latter temple shall be greater than the former,' says the Lord of hosts. 'And in this place I will give peace,' says the Lord of hosts.

The temple had been torn down. There was no reason to see anything other than ruin. Yet, in the midst of ruin and devastation, faith began to arise. Can you breathe in and let faith arise today in you? Your picture may be bleak and desolate. Can you begin, like Haggai, to say, "Though I see only ruin with my natural eyes, my spirit man is taking over. I can see it. I can see the church being restored. I can see businesses prospering. I can see this country coming to Christ. I can see my neighborhood cleaned up and real community happening. I will not believe the lies any longer. I can see the glory of the former temple being restored. I see a place of glory!" *If you can, your thinking is beginning to change!*

Remember, you must be open-handed. It is not your company; It is the Lord's. He is already testing your heart to discover what you will do with the finances. If you don't tithe, I can't see how He can prosper you. Malachi 3 says that the Devourer is rebuked through tithe *and* offerings. I can't envision any prosperity if the Devourer is free to roam in your life. If you want more understanding on tithing, contact me. I would be glad to elaborate. The Bible is so clear on this subject that it would take a book in itself, but I am sure willing to help you if you need help seeing it.

The test is underway. God is looking at how you will handle what He might pour through your hands. Are your hands open? Does it freely flow?

PROVERBS 11:25 — "The generous soul will be made rich, and he who waters will also be watered himself."

When God finds a generous soul, riches are not far behind. We have to assess whether our hands are open for this kind of flow. It's a great question. Think about it as you read the following steps:

1. Assess your area. What will work there? What does not already exist? What does? I can't emphasize this enough: Don't allow your preconceived notions to alter your assessment. In other words, if you have always wanted to open a bakery, but there are several well established bakeries there already, it's probably not the business you should start. Let God give you creative ideas which abound in Him. At this moment, I have some businesses in mind for my area that I *know* would work. Look your area over and find out what the real need is.

2. Ask questions and listen to the responses you receive. This is not only spiritual, but natural as well. Remember, the agenda is not yours; it is the Lord's. Let me quote you something good and necessary: "As the Lord makes His economy more dominant on the world scene, He will define for us how He wants His people to conduct themselves outside the walls of the church house. When our conduct reflects biblical principles, we can expect the engagement of God in a supernatural way. The church house is where we are equipped. The Marketplace is where we share the Gospel. More resources will be coming into the hands of God's people. A greater passion for the cultural change that is required for us conduct ourselves by the standards of the Kingdom is beginning to emerge. So, how does a business owner, a corporate executive, a street vendor, or a government leader tap into this heavenly wisdom:" Author   Unknown

I want to remind you that we accomplish these things by asking questions and by acknowledging that God owns the expertise.

   a. Express the need.
   b. Don't pray about your needs.
      Ask the Lord for His desire.
   c. Seek Him with no agenda.

Ask those who run a kingdom business. Research the Internet. Gather knowledge; it will save you time and money. Ask your pastor and please don't think he is being unspiritual if he tells you *no* because he may be protecting you.

3. Write a plan of action and purpose. How are you going to get there? Dream about one year. Where do you plan to be? Dream about five years. Where do you plan to be then? How will you finance it? This is the biggest question, but it isn't that hard to answer. Think it through on paper. Virtually every bank or lender will want a business plan, so write one. Again, the Internet contains great tools on how to create a business plan. Use them. And put some feet to your plans. If you are unwilling to do this, your business will probably not work. Diligence sees a dream all the way to fruition. Sound difficult? It will cause you to be realistic in your expectations, leaving the rest to God. Do not expect to earn millions right away; it simply won't happen. I made this mistake. Give yourself time, and let God grow the business over time.

4. Work hard and be patient. Accomplishing the vision will take hard work. This is one of the most baffling areas where so many Christians make mistakes. Don't go into this with some "pie in the sky" mentality. You will need to work hard if you're going to start and operate a business

for God. The Scripture is clear on this. Part of the curse is that we will work for what we eat. The New Testament tells us that if we don't work, neither should we eat. You will have to work hard...harder than you have ever worked! The results are worth the effort. Plan on three to five years of sweat; it will likely take that long. If you aren't willing to put forth this kind of effort, don't try it.

5. Be creative in your approach. There is always more than one way to accomplish a plan, and you don't have to work alone. Perhaps you have heard the expression "two heads are a freak" or "too many cooks spoil the soup." Can you imagine that kind of thinking at Compaq™ and Hewlitt Packard™? The maxim "two heads *are* better than one" might better summarize the merger of these two companies. Why do you think the largest companies on our planet merge? It's because they can make more money by uniting.

Could this also be an answer for our churches? Let us look at a typical example. In many areas, one church of 50 people is doing the same things as another church of 50 people only three blocks away. They each have youth groups of eight kids. They pay their bills and struggle to survive. How crazy is that? Could one church of 100 members have greater power, influence, and finances? Why not take a lesson from the world and the Bible (Luke

16:9)? Merge! Be creative. Build relationships that result in win-win situations. In other words, work alongside others to help them grow their church businesses and prosper as you would want them to help you prosper. That's Kingdom thinking. Structure it, of course, but do it. You can work with others and be successful. Every business I have written about has been successful because we worked with others.

Don't let the Enemy deceive you! He does not want your business to work, so he plants negative thoughts in your head that it won't be successful. You must remember to think outside the box about what will benefit everyone, not just yourself. That is the only way God will bless your project.

The main reason I have seen churches fail and not walk in the truth of what I've written about is simple greed. It's amazing that tried-and-true business experience is often rejected because "we can make money doing this ourselves" or "I don't trust that guy" or "why should he make that much money?"

One day, when I was working hard on our Velcro contact, the president of Velcro asked me this question. Kirk, do you want to make ten percent of a million dollars or one hundred percent of nothing? I was trying to negotiate my terms so hard that I almost negotiated myself right

IMPACT

out of the deal of a lifetime. I've seen this over and over and over again. Quite frankly, I believe it is the Enemy trying to stop the Kingdom from advancing. He hates the message of this chapter. The moment the Kingdom really begins to operate in the fashion I have discussed and works together with profits going in all kinds of directions, he will be finished and he knows it. So, he deceives people into mistrust or unsound assumptions to thwart the Kingdom plan that God has in mind.

If you are Kingdom minded, you should want others to succeed. I know I do! I have been mistrusted many time because people thought I must be working some kind of angle. We have to fight greed and its ugly head. Work together...find a way to do it.

In closing, let me breathe faith into you as you read on. God is in charge. It is His Earth, and you are His child. As He is raising you into the ways of the Kingdom, He has one Fatherly plan and that is to bless you. Isn't that the heart of every good father? In the story of the Prodigal Son, who ran away and spent his money foolishly, the father's heart never changed. When he saw his son returning, the father ran down the road to greet him, hug him, and welcome him home. Success in God's Kingdom doesn't hinge upon who you are or what you've done. If you are a part of His Kingdom, He is waiting for you. He rejoices over you with love. He will give you creative ideas. He says, yes, yes, yes! Let's do this together. You have the incredible, indescribable God of all creation on your side. Tap into His ideas. For such a time as this, you have been born.

THE CONCLUSION

I love the story of Chris Gardner. He is the main character in the movie *The Pursuit of Happiness*. Chris had a major obstacle in front of him. He needed to get more clients than all the other brokers. He was trying to beat them out for the one position that was being offered. He needed the job. He needed the money. What Chris did was amazing! He worked relentlessly. He realized that if he didn't hang up his phone, he could cut out eight seconds between phone calls. He realized that if he didn't drink coffee or water, he didn't have to go to the bathroom as often. He made every shortcut he could come up with. He worked as hard as he could. He was passionate about what this would do for his family. Chris got the job and went on to become a multimillionaire.

I would like to pose some questions to the church world. Are you that passionate for the needs of the world? Can you see that your tithes and offerings can change the world around us? Can you see God's simplicity and your obedience are actually world changing? I can't even imagine what heaven will be like when we see the faces of people who were affected by our giving. It will be beyond anything we can imagine here on earth. It can be done, but we can't wait. There are lives that hang in the balance.

I'm reminded of one last story. Mel Gibson, in the film *Braveheart*, was going to give his famous "Sons of Scotland" speech. Others were walking away, not willing to fight, and suddenly William Wallace appears. He begins to address them.

Wallace: "Sons of Scotland, I am William Wallace."

Young soldier: "William Wallace is seven feet tall.

Wallace: Yes, I've heard. Kills men by the hundreds, and if he were here he'd consume the English with fireballs from his eyes and bolts of lightning from his arse. I AM William Wallace. I see a whole army of my countrymen here in defiance of tyranny. You have come to fight as free men and free men you are. What would you do without freedom? Will you fight?"

Veteran soldier: "Fight? Against that? No, we will run; and we will live."

Wallace: Aye, fight and you may die. Run and you'll live, at least for a while. And dying in your beds many years from now, would you be willing to trade all the days from this day to that for one chance, just one chance to come back here and tell our enemies that they may take our lives, but they'll never take our freedom?!"

I want to know, what will we say on our deathbeds? I believe it will primarily be one of two things. We will either say: "The church could have done it, but I lived for myself and my wants and my desires and nothing in this world has really changed" OR "We did it" Veni, vidi, vici. We saw, we came, we conquered! Lives, communities, and the world is changed." The church did it. We were obedient in tithes. We were obedient in offerings. The world is different and they are all praising the God of the church, Jesus.

This is our time! You were born for such a time as this! You are a world-changer! It's not just talk any longer. We have to acknowledge this call and make a difference. The path is simple and well laid out. Let's embrace it! It's time to join the revolution gained by your obedience. It's time to change our communities. It's time to change the world!

42622907R00050

Made in the USA
Middletown, DE
17 April 2017